No End of Vision:

Texas as Seen by Two Laureates

No End of Vision:
Texas as Seen by Two Laureates

Karla K. Morton
2010 Texas Poet Laureate
Photography

Alan Birkelbach
2005 Texas Poet Laureate
Poetry

ISBN 978-0-9827514-7-3
Library of Congress Control Number: 2011923603

Copyright © 2011 Karla Morton, photography; Alan Birkelbach, poetry
All rights reserved
Manufactured in the United States of America

cover photographs by Karla K. Morton
Port Aransas Beach
Palo Duro Canyon

Ink Brush Press
Temple, Texas

For my dear friend Alan,
who always believed in me and my work;
who gave me the confidence to reach for the sun.
                                  Karla K. Morton

For Karla K. Morton, my source of inspiration—
and to all the laureates who came before.

                            Alan Birkelbach

Other books by Karla K. Morton

Wee Cowrin' Timorous Beastie (a 17th Century Scottish Epic book/CD Lagniappe Publishing)
Redefining Beauty (Dos Gatos Press)
Becoming Superman (Zone Press)
Stirring Goldfish (a Sufi poetry book by Finishing Line Press)
Karla K. Morton: New and Selected Works (TCU Press)
Names We've Never Known (The Texas Review Press)

Other books by Alan Birkelbach

Bone Song (Counterpoint Publishing)
Weighed in the Balances (Plain View Press)
No Boundaries (Eakin Press)
Translating the Prairie (City of Plano publisher)
Smurglets are Everywhere (TCU Press)
New and Selected Works (TCU Press)
Rogue Waves (Texas Review Press)
The Thread (Eakin Press)

CONTENTS

Photograph		Poem	
Self-portrait on the San Gabriel, Georgetown	viii	A Third Truth	1
gold in my hands	2	Chrysopaic Spagyria	3
Walking Water	4	Belief	5
Fencing in Palo Duro	6	Fence Line in the Canyon	7
Cactus and a Beetle	8	Destination	10
dancing tree tips	10	Responding As We Know How	11
Old Ford Grill	12	During a Cool, Late Night on Wide Open Highway 287	13
old wheels	14	Old Wheels	15
Guardian Angel	16	Boat Tail Grackle	17
Scrying	18	Scrying	19
Deer Leg	20	What We Set Aside	21
What the Fish Sees	22	Carried by the Styx	23
Where San Antonio Superheroes Shop	24	El Rey de Todos Lagartos	25
San Antonio	26	None Shall Pass	27
street scenes	28	Seductress	29
Sirena of Salado	30	Ben Ficklin Flotsam	31
Jesus Stuff	32	Jesus Stuff	33
Ful-O-Pep	34	All in a Name	35
Horse Monster	36	Inspiration	37
hermit love	38	Sea Love	39
my new boots	40	My New Boots	41
Thank you...Thank you verra much	42	Procession O' Evil	43
too much tomato	44	Prime Heart	45
octopus	46	In the Riverbank	47
Barracuda	48	Barracuda	49
gatorwood	50	What we Truly Are	51
White Head	52	A Dim But Sure Light	53
Old Swings	54	Caesura	55
Woman of the Sky	56	Regal	57
Sponge Bones	58	Examining the Fossil	59
Hay Futures	60	Square Bales and Round	61
chapel	62	Finding the Chapel Out Past Knowing	63
What Emerges	64	In the Desert, Finding the Wall with the Stone Beast	65
West Texas Road Art	66	On the Road to Castaneda	67
Leaving Texas	68	As Far As the Eye	69
Silos—modern Texas art	70	Silos	71
A Moment in Time	72	Good-Bye She Waved Royally	73
What Lifts Us Up	74	What Lifts Us Up	75
Highway, West Texas	76	Stepping Off	77

Self-portrait on the San Gabriel, Georgetown

A Third Truth

A woman raised close to Shafter
has a way of making demands
on men that isn't fair.

There's only two things
she learns to depend on
and neither one is a man.

Rattlesnakes come and go,
roadrunners have no loyalty,
and clouds are fickle as grade-school
friends.

But she knows rocks
and she knows her shadow.
Even if she jumps and clears the ground

she knows neither will leave her.
It's a proven, given thing,
something more sure than her name.

"Can you be as true as this?"
she'll ask a man, pointing to
the darkness at her feet,

and her shadow will make
the point again for her,
challenging the man double.

Few men can stand up to it:
That *this* can be the very stones—
or the indisputable nature of light,

both formidable arguments.
Most men will walk away,
searching for easier game.

But the smartest one
will load her in a pickup
and drive hours out of his way.

He will carry her,
take off her shoes,
make her close her eyes,

Then set her down
in the middle of a shallow river,
where the running water

goes on out of sight.
He will stand behind her
and whisper in her ear,

"Stones." Shadow."
Then he will breathe and say,
"Me."

gold in my hands

Chrysopaic Spagyria

(the alchemic secret of turning plants into gold)

How shall I spend these fine medallions minted fresh?
What grocer, blacksmith, haberdasher will accept
these coins? Here. I give them all to you.
I will fill your pockets, bless your shoes, and wash your hair
with sunlight's true release. You will not need to bite
the scalloped edge to know the metal's worth.
You have changed my heart of wood into a thing
so luminous the sparrows and the starlings float
amazed, afraid the drabness of their song
and dreary wings would diminish such a fiery thing.
Your touch is water, earth, and fire, your breath
the sweetest wind. So now instead of being rooted,
thick and lumpish, I burst, I burst, so you may gather me,
dull into gold, sweet transubstantiation.

Walking Water

Belief

We test the joints
and line up the wheels
like we have sense
and know what we are doing.

In fields bigger
than most men's faith
there's no other answer
than letting the machines do the work.

A mindless army on the move:
when they're running
it's a blessing,
the pipes cool in the hand.

You want to follow along,
be bathed in the mist,
stay holy,
smell the perfume from the rows.

It's prayer we're pumping
up from the aquifer,
believing the blessing is endless,
wanting to stay holy.

So we align the machines
let them carry our hopes,
spraying our wishes out
farther than we can see.

Fencing in Palo Duro

Fence Line in the Canyon

A fence here can't have ambition.
It's tough enough to sink a post,
chewing through the rock
to set up for a false order.

These wide-open rails
will only turn the thickest of beasts.
It's not a land for souls
who measure things in days and months.

Distance is all about perspective;
even if the fence-row runs
beyond sight and into the waves of heat.
It doesn't keep out time.

The agarita won't care, the rabbitbush will stand aloof,
and the spiny yucca will maintain its watch;
their roots have touched the lips of fossils,
plan or no plan, fence or no fence.

Eventually this country will claim these posts,
bring them down and embrace them in hot sleep.
Some other road might come through;
the goldenrod will baptize its transience.

In the meantime, we stay on this side,
sure that over there is something burning and wild,
maybe some new eras of rattlesnakes, full of spike and spittle,
angry we crossed over to watch them be born.

cactus and a beetle

Destination

I do not see his Virgil here,
climbing backward up this green terrain.
And there are no small, miserable sinners
impaled on their own misery.

Perhaps this is not about overturned theology at all.
This might be how bugs view the world:
a flat geography, one surface after another—
It is all the same to them. There are no lessons
other than maneuvering around yucca, cholla,
and fleshy nodes.

I am not omniscient here. But neither
do I interfere. He has his steps
and I have mine and they have led
me here to watch. Is he watching me in turn,
deciding if he will have to navigate
around my boat-like foot?

Even the smallest leg has faith.
His journey might not end
when he climbs up to solid ground,
or mine when I detour around
this succulent.

We step. We step again
forward into our geography,
held confident and secure
by the great spatulate hand of God.

dancing tree tips

Responding As We Know How

An oak isn't prone to dance.
It would rather maintain
a certain dignity.
It has a narrow mind

against caprice. Not like a
wiry mesquite whose heart
thrives on neglect but who
will still shoot roots along

a twisted path. More like a
matron elm than the lank
limbs of a cypress or
gyrated juniper.

A routine thing would not have
been enough. No northern
wind with icy tunes, no
storm with harsh timpanies.

This oak must know those sounds well.
But sweeter music played.
Something penetrated
this barkish consciousness.

You must have passed by here, notes
on your lips, a little
hummed nothing. Maybe you
waded in the shallows,

the stream rilling over your
playful toes. Maybe the
oak felt the vibrations
from your porcelain feet.

Or maybe, just maybe, this
oak tree began dancing
to the sweet song of your
voice as you blessed each root,

flower, stone, and wondrous beast.
Oh, let me dance here, too.
Your breath will guide my breath.
Your heart will set my heart.

Old Ford Grill

During a Cool, Late Night Drive on Wide-Open Highway 287

We reach for each other's hand across the seat,
and talk, and dare to peer in the rearview mirrors,
looking back over our shoulder,
hoping to see our racing youth of an old Ford pickup:
the gaping maws of our omniverous mouths,
two round eyes brightly staring,
white metal teeth
chewing up our roads

old wheels

Old Wheels

They would not be playing dominoes
even if they knew how.
To them the world was all motion
or not. They always depended on gravity or horsepower
and they held on to that faith.
There was no question:
the world was a plane;
there was no worry about horizon
or destination. There was only the now of rolling
or not. One day they quit moving,
but they are sure they could still roll along
if they were just given
a push.

Guardian Angel

Boat-tail Grackle

There's nothing from the sea that scares him.
It's a geography he does not consider.
The gulls and cormorants are bullies;
they let him know in no uncertain terms
he's not welcome, the waves and what they bring
are not for him. He's not too full of pride
for tactical retreat, even if it's not his native demesne.
He'll go this far and no farther.
Don't try to muscle him away. Somehow he
knows the soldier's innate sense of fitting into
a castle's line, the security of a body's symmetry
to structure. He walks the deck like a sentry.
You almost expect to catch him leaning on a spear,
watching the sky for threat,
the sunlight reflecting off the bead of his eye.

Scrying

Scrying

There is no end of vision
to a well-tuned eye.
A thing cannot reflect more than it is,
but all the things it can be are there.

To a well-tuned eye.
there is more than just now.
Everything that can be is there
in the bowl, in the water, in the next breath.

There is more than just now,
more than just ourselves,
in the bowl, in the water, in the next breath.
We should pay attention, watch how things transform.

More than just ourselves
there is stone and water and blossom.
We should pay attention, watch how things transform
It is imperative.

Here is stone and water and blossom.
A thing will always reflect more than it is
Look. It is a divine imperative.
There is no end of vision.

Deer Leg

What We Set Aside

We don't use the word *hasten* anymore.
It isn't lost—just neglected.

In the sidewalk down the street
someone left a footprint in the cement when it was wet.
Maybe farther down there is a date, a star,
a big heart with an arrow through it.
"M.H. loves C.S."
We are all changed moment to moment.
What were we before the concrete called to us?

We do not think anything of finding
a nail, a pencil, even a shoe in the street,
a pair of glasses, the tiny hands from a watch.
Now where have those people gone?
Have they been transformed?

My grandfather could read the hieroglyphic tracks
that animals would scratch in the dirt.
He could tell me when the animal had come through,
which direction they were heading,
how quickly they were running.

Around each corner of time
is a new adventure, maybe a mark we can leave,
an artifact of our old selves we can shed,
a skin we can molt, a price we are willing to pay.

What discovery, what joy
might yet tear us apart.

Over there I hear someone
bathing behind the bushes.
Who knows how long they will be there.
We should hurry.
We should hasten.

What the Fish Sees

Carried by the Styx

A flooded creek does not discriminate.
It will tote anything in its urgency.
Hurry, it will say, hurry.
We have an appointment downstream.

A body left loose, neglected,
or not paying attention
will get swept up and scoured,
regardless of what it might have been doing.

It's always best to watch a storm
from under a roof.
Out exposed on uneven ground
you feel like you're tempting Fate

whether you mean to or not.
Mad water will carry any soul
to unknown destinations,
stopping time with the roiling.

But, eventually, everything succumbs to mud.
Tomorrow we'll be wiping dust again
and counting heads, wondering how far we'll
have to travel to make things complete.

Something bigger than us
will sweep us one day,
something in a rush,
with its own blinding endpoint.

Until then we ride the dry arroyos,
hours behind the vultures,
the last few of all our dreams
cupped in our eyes.

Where San Antonio Superheroes Shop

El Rey de Todos Lagartos

Larger than life, in pink and green leotards,
they stride the brick streets like colossus,
upholding la ley, protecting the weak,
bringing milk to the mothers,
delivering masa, even cold cerveza:
los ángeles en la noche

El Diablo.
El Tigre de Fuego.
El Rey de Todos Lagartos.

I have seen them,
leaping through the glow of yellow porch lights,
their capes like flags.

And when they are tired,
when they cannot run another alleyway,
when mere mortal threads are worn through,
when they cannot sew another stitch
then they come here.

They come here, to my window:
a package arrives holding money
with instructions:
"Please leave the mask for El Caballo Dorado
outside your back door.
Vaya con dios."
So I do,
and in the morning the mask is gone.

The next time I need salve
for my knees and tired hands
there, in my window,
it will appear, alongside
a small, plastic lizard.

I leave him there
as a guardian in stead.

San Antonio

None Shall Pass

Steadfast and iron-shod
he is prepared to blow his horn
at anyone who dares to attempt
to enter the Golden Arches.

Where was he when I got married
the first time? He could have
chained himself across the church aisle,
made the flower girls trip over him.

With hair and beard as stiff as wire,
and fingers down to the line,
it's a sure bet he's seen his share
of personal choice disasters:

Used car lots, bad barbecue places,
three-card-monty boxes,
faith healers, street vendors,
suspicious taquerias.

Should I step this way,
should I eat there,
is this ring real gold?
Just hesitate—and he will be there

between you and the outcome,
blaring and blasting.
Look, his horn will say,
Another fool!

And all the public will turn and stare
as you become ashamed of fries,
humbled by happy meals,
made contrite by dubious fish sandwiches.

Street Scenes

Seductress

She stands in the doorway
and looks at me
out of the corner of her eye

Seducing me
with her toothless grin,
one eye tilts up,
promising mischief.

I believe
she might have a chaw
tucked
into her lower lip.

Her look hints that
she can sell me
a telephone,
any electronics I want
in case I would ever
want to call her

sometime when there
is no traffic,
when I am alone
and lonely,
when it is night.

She suggests
she would only leave her hat on
if I asked.

Sirena of Salado

Ben Ficklin Flotsam

I need a house somewhere
on a high bank
of the South Concho,
higher even
than the stone remnants
of the Ben Ficklin Courthouse,
a house so high it takes
six seconds,
maybe more,
for the dopplered bawl
of any deluge-borne calf
to reach me,
and well out of range
of any errant
mossy mermaid
who might have been
displaced and
left behind
during any
unexpected Biblical
flood.

Jesus Stuff

Jesus Stuff

If only all signs
were always this clear.

When you boil a religious metaphor
down to its ester

usually you're left with something
that looks suspiciously like burnt toast,

or old, dried apricot,
or hair-sprayed rose petal.

Which isn't to say
such things aren't holy,

surely as holy, at least,
as a spilled bag of grass clippings,

or floating letters in a bowl of generic cereal.
But that's what people don't get:

about how the mundane can be holy,
about how stuff can be said right out loud,

about how bringing up his name
can be common as hardscrabble,

about how just about everything
is about Jesus,

and how it's perfect for it to be next to objects
that shine, shine, shine.

Ful-O-Pep

All in a Name

You learn to depend on some things:
August won't bring rain,
any rose that survives its first summer
will outlive you;

leftover minnows in the watering trough
aren't fast enough for nocturnal raccoons;
the wind always brings in
more sand than you can sweep;

the deep-down name of things doesn't change.
Stones, even if they walk at night,
are still stones; mesquite thorns,
regardless of exclamation, will still pierce a boot.

Animals will always come in for food,
(and if they don't that's a darker truth).
Three scoops for each dog
and a heaping bucket for the questing chickens.

Like they could read the title
on the bag, they seem as happy
as if each meal was the first and best,
what they've waited their lives for.

I know the true name for the vivifying lock
that falls across my wife's blue eyes.
And she has the perfect word she calls me
when I kiss her neck at night.

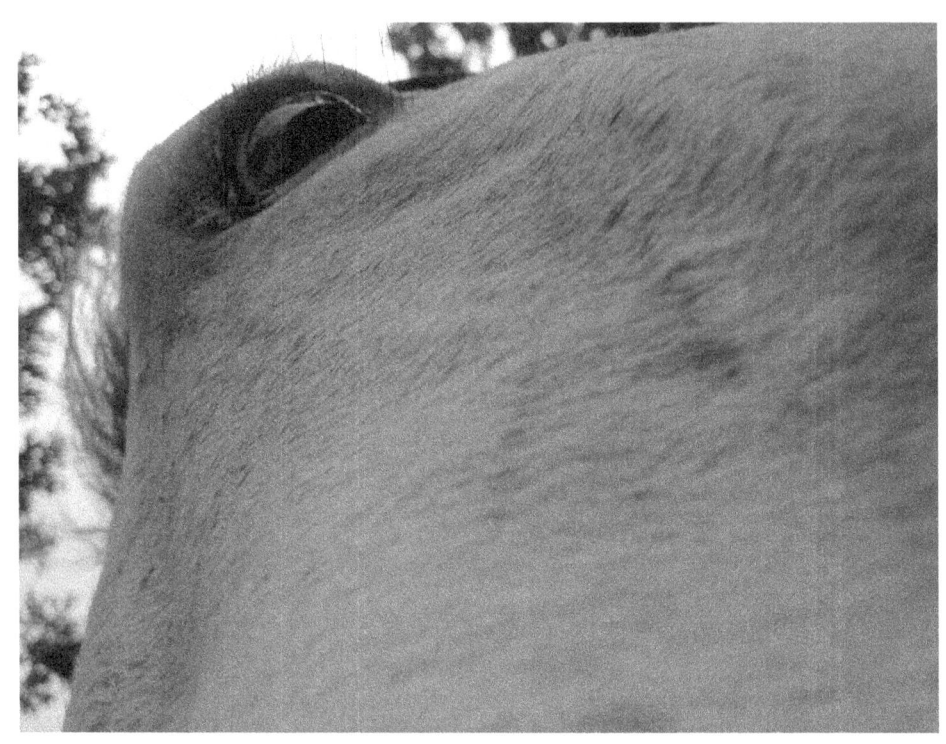

horse monsters

Inspiration

It came to us in a dream, of course:
the odd angle of vision, the vast plain of
his head leading to the omniscient eye.
Based on what we see he must have emerged whole,
bypassing the awkwardness of being a foal,
no bony leaping or testing of the mane.
Maybe he was only a god in transition,
towering over us, freshly borne from
a more base shape like a fish, a tree,
canes clacking by a river. What shivered
his muscles, what bare limbs caused his
heart to race, what charge triggered in his brain
to mold into this shape? What fire
flared from his nostrils, what turf like clouds
sped beneath his barreled chest?
What springs might yet burst forth
called by his raging hooves?

hermit love

Sea Love

As brazen as they are
still I admire them.
They have met at their sandy assignation,
pulled their chitinous blankets around,
and decided the world can wait.

This is a confidence
in passion most to be
admired. Regardless of how waves might sweep them,
or some larger tread or claw might come
along, still they have no need to

be invisible. They
hold their pearly kiss, as
oblivious to our eyes as to time. It
is almost too intimate to watch,
their briny, green imperative.

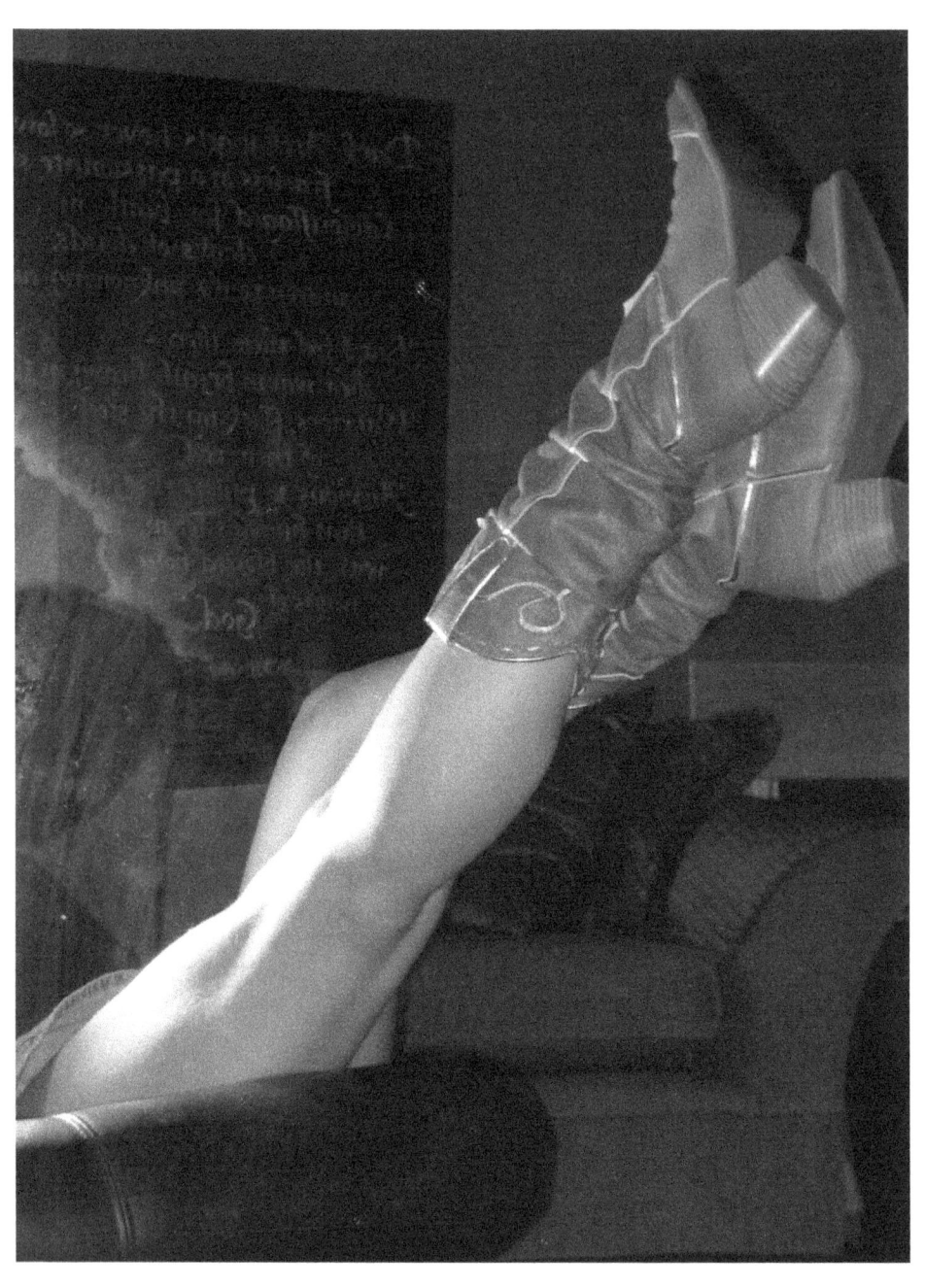

my new boots

My New Boots

I'm here to show you my new boots.
I'm filled with such delight
I had to stop and share my joy.
I hope that that's alright.

Look at that heel, that stitch, that vamp.
They make you want to stare.
Oh, tell me truly—have you ever
seen a finer pair?

What's that? I should wear jeans with boots?
That shows how much you know.
You wouldn't see the boots at all—
or how far up they go.

You should have seen my mama's boots
when she was in her prime.
Since she's not here I hope my boots
will help you pass the time.

I'm here to show you my new boots,
the best I can recall.
They're light as clouds; I feel like I
have nothing on at all.

Here. Let me kick a little bit
and point a perfect toe.
These brand-new boots are aching for
a well-led do-si-do.

You might not be a gentleman.
You've let your eyeballs stray.
And after all my work to put
these beauties on display!

My eyes are blue as prairie sage.
My hair grows wild and free.
But I'm just here to show my boots.
That's all you get to see.

Thank you . . . Thank you verra much

Procession O' Evil

> A daemonibus doctuture, de daemonibus doctet, et ad darmones ducit*

When it comes
to a wagonload of trouble
Elvis probably has to wheel
in somewhere after a
hootchie-coochie piñata
of Little Egypt
(with little paper flurries
covering the best parts)
and just slightly before
a hot, bubbling cart
full of Frito Pie.
But the best Evil provokes
it's own unique kind
of delicious reaction:
every man this wagon passes
will try to sneer,
will go, "Uh-huh-huh,"
will try to move his overage hips,
will call his girlfriend Priscilla at least once,
and will daydream of a Red Ryder full
of tissue, teenage girls
following in his wake.

It is taught by the demons, it teaches about demons, and it leads to demons
—Albertus Magnus

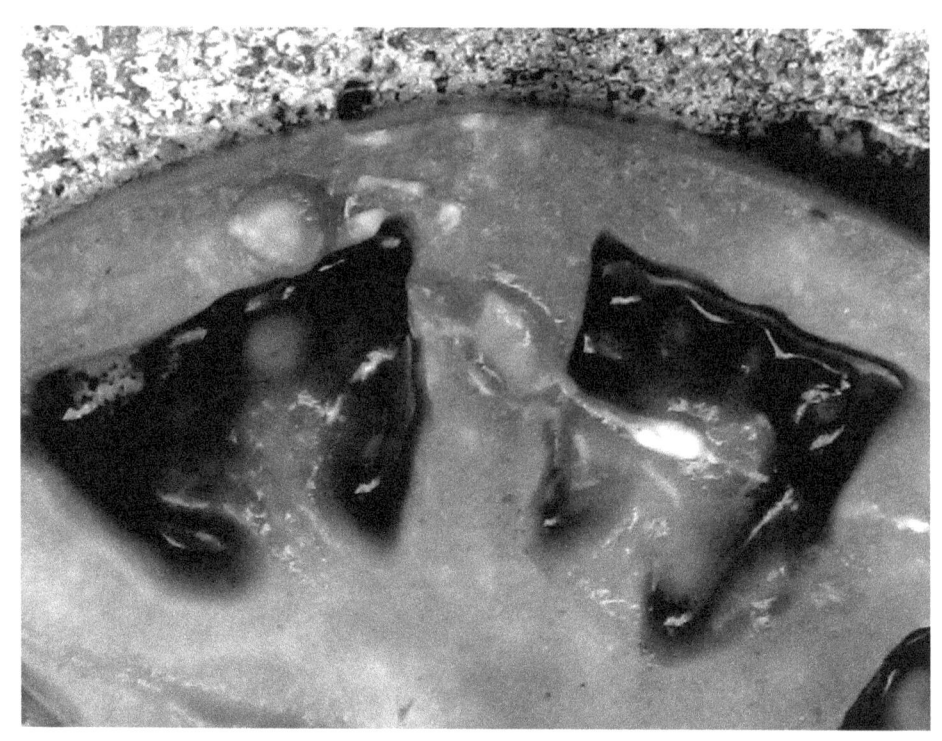

too much tomato

Prime Heart

It is the terrible perfection
of its symmetry that gives us pause.
It seems there is no end
to it, a cathedral that

is never done. How fleshy might it
yet get, its meat still quivering from
providential cause? What
triggered this heart to beat,

the moist chambers to pulse? To create
such a dichotomous thing from such
a base origin, to
culture from the darkest

reviled root this bilateral beast
requires a wise and careful mover.
It governs structure deep,
and deeper still, beyond

histology, past disposition,
when we are finally torn, and torn again
in half, our heart laid bare
exposed, all too aware

of that galvanic machinery
that powers all, our meager spark, our
pure connectedness, our
dreadful anatomy.

octopus

In the Riverbank

Something
has been earthed there.
The ground will roil
beneath your feet.

It will burst upon you unexpected in your sleep,
extract you from your sleeping bag,
limbs clacking and fibrous,
a wooden beak, moss and silt slavering.

It is a thing far more terrible,
and far less laborious
than an errant angry turtle
or a common lungfish.

Around a campfire
this is not the story people tell—
tubers weaving around them like a mantle,
stones for jaws.

They do not have conspiratorial whispers
of anything like this,
nothing that tests their friable nature,
their ability to breathe underground.

Barracuda

Barracuda

No matter where you stand
his eyes will follow you—

like the picture of Jesus
in your grandmother's house

where over there was the chalk dog
and over there was the console television

and hanging over there was the picture of Jesus
with the recessed eyes and the straight lips.

At least in some paintings of Jesus,
even the paint-by-number Last Supper,

you could imagine him blinking,
and it was all about staring at him.

But with grandma's Jesus he always made it about you.
A boy couldn't watch a cartoon without being judged.

A person ended up trying to align every football game
with the seven deadly sins.

Those eyes made you question everything you did:
vacuuming the rug, washing dishes, dusting,

making the bed—everything domestic and banal
and common, even something as simple

as the sun, a light fishing rig, ten-pound test line,
and a smooth surf that shouldn't contain such terror.

gatorwood

What We Truly Are

This is the story of the alligator
who one day lifted both left legs
then both right legs
out of the swampy-swamp
and chose free will over frogs.

Immediately being discontent
he asked God (who is reptilian after all)
to be made into some other thing
that might be more satisfying
while still retaining some of the croc-y nature.

God ticked off his fingers, ruled out
manhole covers and steam shovels
and mailboxes and grills on old cars
and he told the alligator that he could
change him into wood.

"Are you sure?" God asked.
He warned the alligator. "There are
no backsies or do-overs.
Once you're wood—you're wood
and there it is."

But the alligator was sure so
poof—and the alligator was wood.
Simple story. Sometimes we ask for help
or direction and it comes down to
the consequences of choice.

We cross a specific street,
stir a pot counter-clockwise,
stick our finger in the wrong pie,
let the marshmallow catch on fire.
Are we sure, are we sure?

There is only, ultimately,
left foot then right foot
until we can't anymore.
We are wood. And air. And full of choice.
Sooner or later someone steps on us.
No more. And never, gloriously, any less.

white head

A Dim But Sure Light

He harbors a dull yearning
that we won't expect
a hereford to look back,
as if extra intelligence
will give him a disguise,
make us think he's a horse
or large, knobbly dog.
Eventually his desire for feed
will give him away, though,
his slot at the trough
overriding any dim, curious spark.
But the fact can't be ignored
that all of us, knowing all predetermined Fates,
were still looking at each other.
Who's to say that one day
walking across a shouldered street,
or boarding a steaming train,
we might hang back on our well-worn path
and see off in the distance
a face staring at us?
The eyes will be open with wonder,
the head slighty tilted, trying to understand,
wondering, intrigued we were still reachable,
our feet hesitant,
our face haloed by hope.

Old Swings

Caesura

A suspended chain will sing to itself.
Even a rope has a melody
if it's left to hang alone.

A man surrounded by quiet
pulls things together. That's just what he does.
He'll load a barrow of rocks
and put them in an edge line
along a flat driveway, marking nothing but space.
He'll try to make a fence straight,
hammering through stone if he has to.

He's trying to impose order, to reduce
the potential of out-of-place noise.
Rain made thick and waxy-sounding
through the yucca is okay.
Something old and reptilian
scuttering through the hardscrabble
is at least right for this lost corner
of the universe.

Some things, though, can't help but make noise,
sing even, if prodded by the wind.
A man can't align everything.
God gave some things an anatomy
perfect for a melody a human will never know.
Spiny branches clack and twine,
cords bind together just so,
rust grooves out a rut,
evening out a tune.

Man can try to corral,
make things quiet by gathering,
but there's a bigger mind at play here,
and better at it.

No road lasts forever.
Sooner or later a fencepost
falls out of measure,
the sinews and grinding gears of all bodies
go back to where they belong,
pulling together with their own gravity,
their hearts slowing down
to sing in a larger chorale.

Woman of the Sky

Regal

As bound by her
protean desire
as any fickle,
teenage girl,
she still maintains
her orgulous demeanor.

She bends but little.
She shreds the wind
with her hair.
She showers her sycophants
with guerdons
of acorns.

There is nothing
between her and the sun:
exactly what she
would expect,
being Queen of her
Diurnal realm.

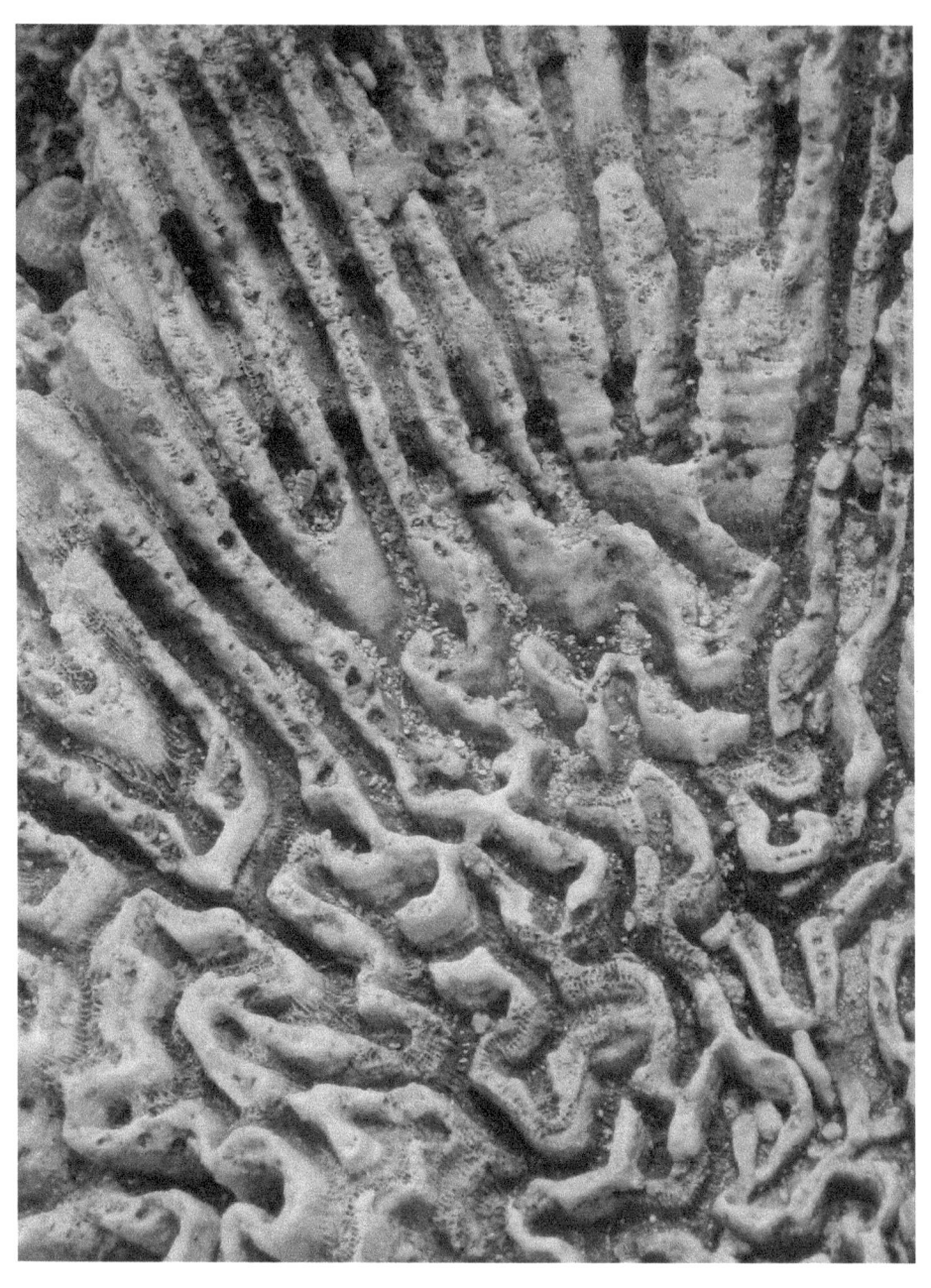

Sponge Bones

Examining the Fossil

If we dared to rub our hands on it
it would certainly seem static.
Ossification has stopped all movement,
even our breathing.
We try to imagine this creature's last stirring.

We might as well sit and stare
at the whorls of our fingers.
wondering if there was a labryinth there
that would lead us
to an enlightment we could not see.

The same currents that shaped our hands
have also draped these fronds.
There is no need to call on it.
It is always around us, blessing us,
keeping things secure.

In the bones of saints
there may yet be the vibrations of prayers.
A chip, a shard, a mote of dust
might contain the ability to heal, to cast away,
to renew.

A flame has burned in every creature.
We should have a map that tells us
where every saint is buried.
For all our occupations
there should be someone who intercedes.

We slap brutish on the stones
that cover and cover deeper
the bones that lie beneath us,
the glistening, ageless miracles
only sleeping beneath our feet.

Hay Futures

Square Bales and Round

When the world is small and square
    and bound
you can lift and place it like bricks,
plan your calendar toward the back
    wall
of the barn, stack the months in
    place.

The higher you go toward the roof
you'll find muscles you didn't know
    you had.
Your gloves will get black creases
    from the wire
and your face will get leafed with
    dust.

There, you'll say, there. It's done.
You can walk away from what
    you've stacked,
close the door, park the tractor,
shake, start dispersing tomorrow.

You'll always worry about snakes,
but they're a known thing.
They'll lair down into a cozy spot,
maybe six or seven rows deep,

and silently put in an alarm
daring you to disturb them
a month down the road.
They don't mind waiting.

Still, it's a condition you can plan
    for
even if it never occurs.
Round bales, though, take that
    certainty away,
bundle it up into a knot too big.

You can't lift them without
    mechanics.
You can't store them personally.
You can't know you've touched
    each one
at least twice, maybe three times,
    yourself.

And the eye will get drawn into the
    spiral.
You'll try to read both the past and
    the future.
You won't be able to help it.
You'll try to change your calendar
    from square to circle—

It won't work. It's too late.
You'll get lost in in the maelstrom,
realize you might have
placated the wrong gods.

You're too old now to go
where the spiraling grass might
    take you.
You'll yearn for the horror of a
    twisting Scylla
over a dread Charybdis.

chapel

Finding the Chapel Out Past Knowing

Somebody's been here before us
and assumed we might need saving.
Or protection at the very least.
In case we just had to go farther.

Maybe they went there and came back.
Every cross implies a 'what happens next.'
"If you open this gate and go on
then all we can offer is words."

It's a sin, this wanting to see past the horizon.
It's the greed of knowing,
the gluttony of over there,
the pride of thinking we can survive anything

We can't know what fangs live under stones,
how quickly we could boil,
how distance gets deeper than God's eyes,
how the thorns might prick our flesh.

This chapel calls us to prayer one last time
when we just have to keep going.
We whisper, asking for a path for the horses,
and a high place to go when the water gets too deep.

What Emerges

In the Desert, Finding the Wall with the Stone Beast

It emerges from the wall
as if in pursuit,
its jaws open, the nape
of its neck bristled thick,

so high off the ground it must
have been flying, or
at least leaping, dead-set
on something time has gnawed

the bones of. This is something
much more savage and
raw than a long-limbed beast
from Babylonian

walls. This is something Nature
carved then discarded,
knowing Man would someday
use the spark of his fears

to quicken it. Here is proof
some things are meant to
only live in darkness.
They cannot stand the Light.

West Texas Road Art

On the Road to Castaneda

the land is as flat
as last year's calendar.
People that live at the foot of mountains,
or close to the ocean,
don't get the way the horizon
can boil the essence of things down.
You know the steel of the railroad
doesn't bend but if you sight an eye
along the track you would still swear
that the metal gentles into a curve,
hugging the earth.
When trains disappear over the edge
the smoke still hangs in the air,
lets you know you aren't there yet
and that there is still a pretty good ways away.
You get a vision that makes you think
you can see through things, through road,
through dirt, through time—
into wherever that train has gone.
Before you even get there
another train will come and go—
yes, it's that far.
And all you want is a simple sign.
You don't need a twisted mesquite pointing the way
or a line of dull-witted cattle.
Maybe you just want some mileage signs
with numbers counting down,
the clouds parting in a welcoming way
over the asphalt,
or a big word written somewhere
that says, simply,
you are still on track.

Leaving Texas

As Far As the Eye

A road should not show more
than a mind can handle.
If it does, then it can't be trusted.
Thank God for curvature. Twelve miles,
fifteen if you're high enough,
is near enough vista to fill the eye.
If you are coming off a plateau
then it might be thirty miles or more.
You'll think you can see
clear through New Mexico,
dropping off into a bowl
with Colorado for a rim.
It will almost be too much
for comprehension, seeing that far out,
a peek into tomorrow,
being aware of where the road
is going to take you.
That's why God smudges that edge
no matter how tall you are.
No geographic psychic can see through it.
It'll change by the time
you get there anyway.
Be content with as far
as your looking goes.
There's more than enough adventures
between here and there.
As you step forward
that horizon will step with you,
and it will drop you off in places
you daren't imagine.

Silos—modern Texas art

Silos

It trembles the mind to think of so much plenty.
The height, like a church steeple,
defies perspective. The silos are so big
you're always thinking you must be getting closer—
but you aren't. You try to measure with a wide eye:
yup—they can hold more
than the flat fields that surround you.
It's an implied abundance
only heard of in the bible.
You might never see it for real and true.
Neither might your children.
Even up close, even covered
with the grain dust raining down,
you think Heaven must be like this,
exactly like this:
ramparts that only stop when they want to—
and still more sky beyond.

A Moment in Time

Good-Bye She Waved Royally

Trying not to enjoy too much
her hand and arm
dipping in the breeze
she laid her head against the cushion
and shut her eyes.

Drivers going the opposite direction
would wave back in salute
wondering
who was that woman
who thought she was queen.

She imagined she was
traveling incognito,
hair pulled up tight,
no glistening, gold-flecked make-up,
no shoes tied by servants.
Only slappy sandals

and faded shorts
and a print shirt
to help her blend in
among the pick-ups and discount stores.

Ah, she had loved the way the heat
had bounced honestly
from the asphalt,
no umbrella to shield her,
no carpet, no patent leathers.
She had bent over once
and put her cheek down to it,
felt the rumble of traffic
like a heartbeat.

From a souvenir shop
she had bought
a trinket of a ring
with a green, glass stone,
a stone the color of the ocean.
the color of her eyes.
It was a bauble she was sure
would make men swoon.

She had sat on the sand,
pretended the diced shells
were rose petals,
let the worshipping waves
kiss her feet.

And now she was waving
goodbye, goodbye,
breathing in the esters
carried to her
by the wind,
her arm,
sitting on the car's window,
dipping up and down
like a dolphin
or some other
royal fish.

What Lifts Us Up

What Lifts Us Up

Our intention is to tell you tales you know but
may have forgotten, not just to tell you tales
of bodies changed to different forms. The world is full
of extraordinary things. In all the seasons,
landscapes, fruit, and sleeping objects, mineral and
vine there is a story and a story and a
story if you know where to look. I will help you
turn a stone. You will help me climb a fence. When you
meet something new say its name twice: once to know it,
once to love it. Trade stories. There is always light
and order; you can lead each other there. Here. Reach.
There is so much to see. There are photos and words.
The world is bursting with stories that will lift you.
Something may say your name twice. See if you are changed.

Highway, West Texas

Stepping Off

Some stories start before this point
but our journey starts here.
Aren't we lucky? We're doing it together.

Look at this blank slate.
Only a few people ever get this chance.
We don't know what we'll end up doing

but the direction is clear.
It's where we've been led.
Can you see it now?

Starting today it's the road and trust.
I'll depend on your vision.
You can listen to my steady heart at night.

We may fall but we have to have faith
there will always be something
to lift us up.

Karla K. Morton, the 2010 Texas Poet Laureate, is a graduate of Texas A&M University and a board member of the Greater Denton Arts Council. A Betsy Colquitt Award winner and Indie National Book Award winner, she has been widely published in literary journals and is the author of six books of poetry. She has been featured on television, radio (NPR) and newspapers across the USA. A native Texan, Morton has trekked thousands of miles for her Little Town, Texas Tour, bringing her poetry and art into schools, colleges, universities, civic groups, cancer support groups, and festivals in communities across her beloved state.

Alan Birkelbach, a native Texan, was the 2005 Poet Laureate of Texas. His work has appeared in journals and anthologies such as *Grasslands Review, Borderlands, The Langdon Review,* and *Concho River Review*. He has received a Fellowship Grant from the Writer's League of Texas, was nominated for a Wrangler, Spur, and Pushcart Prizes, and is a member of The Academy of American Poets. He has eight collections of poetry: *Bone Song, Weighed in the Balances, No Boundaries, New and Selected Works, Translating the Prairie, Smurglets Are Everywhere, Rogue Waves,* and *The Thread*. His latest project is serving as editor for the volume *Dark Inspiration: The Poetry of Robert E. Howard.*

www.ingramcontent.com/pod-product-compliance
Lightning Source LLC
Chambersburg PA
CBHW031207090426
42736CB00009B/809